Written by Kelly Hargrave
Designed by Ali Castro and Brie Nagy
Illustrated by Brie Nagy
Beast Photography by Left Side Down

Tangerine
Press
an imprint of
SCHOLASTIC
www.scholastic.com

Scholastic and Tangerine Press and associated logos are trademarks and/or registered trademarks of Scholastic Inc. Published by Tangerine Press, an imprint of Scholastic Inc., 557 Broadway, New York, NY 10012

10 9 8 7 6 5 4 3 2 1

ISBN: 978-1-338-03342-7

Scholastic Inc.
New York, NY

Scholastic Australia Pty. Ltd.
Gosford, NSW

Scholastic Canada Ltd.
Markham, Ontario

Scholastic New Zealand Ltd.
Greenmount, Auckland

CONTENTS

EPIC BATTLE OF THE AGES

Get ready, myth mavens and legend lords! This book is full of fearsome facts of two fantastical beasts that might never have crossed paths in real life, but with this book and kit, you will have the chance of the ages to let your imagination run wild when these two beasts come together for a deadly duel.

With the information we've packed in these pages, you will find out what makes a battle between the magical dragon and the mythical griffin so epic. And best of all, you will have a chance to craft your own griffin and dragon out of clay using the skeletons provided. Then use the included poster as a backdrop to stage your own legendary battle scenes.

Dragons and griffins are amazing creatures that have been both feared and admired throughout the greater western world, especially during medieval times. Each mythical beast has incredible powers and ultra-awesome strengths!

There are countless of stories of humans, heroes, and gods encountering these beasts, but what would happen if a dragon and griffin came face-to-face?

Would it be a gruesome and bloodthirsty fight to the death, or would it be a whimsical, witty, and entertaining encounter? All of the exciting and epic details are right here in this one-of-a-kind book!

INCLUDED IN THIS KIT

- ✠ *Mythical Beasts* Book
- ✠ Dragon Skeleton
- ✠ Griffin Skeleton
- ✠ Air-Dry Clay
- ✠ Metallic Glaze
- ✠ Paintbrush
- ✠ Poster

DRAGON vs. GRIFFIN

WELCOME TO THE MOST EXCITING HEAD-TO-HEAD BATTLE IN MYTHOLOGICAL BEAST HISTORY! NO HUMAN HAS EVER WITNESSED A BATTLE BETWEEN A GRIFFIN AND DRAGON—UNTIL NOW!

According to mythology from around the world, dragons have a mixed reputation— from loyal and wise guardians to annoying but magical nuisances to feared, fire-breathing destroyers. Dragons are also known to be treasure hunters and hoarders.

A guardian and protector of priceless possessions, the powerful, divine, and majestic griffin is known as the king of all beasts.

If the dragon is a treasure hunter and the griffin is a treasure guardian, what do you think will happen when these two amazing beasts come face-to-face?

The only way you will be able to know is if you closely examine each beast: its natural habits, special abilities, amazing strengths, and unfortunate weaknesses against the other. You may think you already know which one will win, but let's see which beast you pick at the end.

THE WINNER WILL KEEP THEIR LIFE AND WIN THE TREASURE.

LET THE BOLD BATTLE FOR THE GOLD BEGIN!

Which beast is destined to win this battle and how?

THE GIFTED GRIFFIN
KING OF LAND AND SKY

The mighty griffin is a top competitor ready for action! It has the body and hind legs of a lion and the head, wings, and talons of an eagle. As a king of both land and the sky, it is a fierce force to reckon with!

The griffin is respected by all who encounter it, but don't expect to be fast friends. The griffin often protects beautiful and very important treasures, so it first needs to make sure you are not a threat.

The griffin is incredibly loyal to what it is protecting, so you had better have a good reason for braving its presence. If you make one wrong move, the griffin won't hesitate to grab you by its talons, fly you across the world, and drop you in the middle of a desert so that you never find your way out.

A griffin knows that many ferocious creatures seek to take its precious treasure. It has developed keen instincts, and it senses surprise attacks from miles away. With special moves to bring down a dangerous predator, the dragon had better watch out! If a dragon wants the griffin's treasure, a bloody battle is sure to take place.

TREASURES GUARDED BY GRIFFINS

- ☒ Gold
- ☒ Gemstones
- ☒ Thrones
- ☒ special treasure that keeps you young forever (what some may call immortal). how cool is that?

7

GRIFFIN LEGENDS

ALL HAIL THE MIGHTY GRIFFIN!

strongest and boldest beast

The griffin is a heroic mythical beast that deserves to be honored. Here are some of the many exciting stories, legends, and artifacts that show how much people worshiped and loved the griffin.

MEDIEVAL MADNESS

In medieval times, the griffin was a popular icon throughout the western world! If it was a student at your school, it would win awards for:

the most respected beast

most likely to have **divine** power

most likely to grow up to be a leader or a king

Because the griffin was an all-around powerful, respected, and cool creature, people used its image as an **emblem** to represent their families, armies, and lands. Griffin images were placed on:

- knights armor
- shields
- seals
- crests
- ships

Alice in Wonderland by Lewis Carroll

A griffin is ordered by the crazy Queen of Hearts to take Alice to see Mock Turtle. Here is an image of Lewis Carroll's "gryphon" drawn by Sir John Tenniel:

The Griffin by the Brothers Grimm

In this creepy, weird story, a young boy visits a griffin's home in order to retrieve one of its magical feathers to give to a king in return for his daughter's hand in marriage. How terrifyingly romantic!

Alexander the Great

Alexander flew on a mighty griffin for seven days to the edge of the sky! Some say he wanted to get a peek at heaven.

9

A griffin can be anywhere from the size of an average lion, which is about 6 ft. (1.8 m) long, all the way up to 48 ft. (14.6 m) long! That is the same size as a humpback whale! Can you imagine a griffin the size of a humpback whale? Some reports say that griffins can have the strength of up to one hundred eagles.

That dragon had better hope it comes across a smaller griffin, because a griffin the size of a humpback whale could kill it with a single belly flop! Check out all the other fearsome features a griffin brings to the battlefield.

GRIFFIN EARS ARE LONG AND STAND UP STRAIGHT, ALWAYS READY TO HEAR WHAT'S GOING ON AROUND IT.

A HOOKED BEAK HELPS THE GRIFFIN RIP THROUGH PREY EASILY. THAT BEAK IS NOTHING TO JOKE ABOUT. IT COULD PROBABLY SLICE THROUGH A T.REX'S BELLY IN A MATTER OF SECONDS!

X SHARP, HOOKED BEAK

X FEATHERY HEAD OF AN EAGLE

X FRONT TALONS OF AN EAGLE

THE AVERAGE GRIFFIN CLAW IS AS LARGE AS AN ANTELOPE HORN, WHICH CAN BE MORE THAN A FOOT (30.48 CM) LONG!

Ӿ EARS OF
A LION

Ӿ WINGS OF
AN EAGLE

A GRIFFIN'S
WINGSPAN CAN
REACH UP TO 25 FT.
(7.6 M), WHICH IS
MUCH LONGER THAN
AN AVERAGE
EAGLE'S
WINGSPAN OF
8 FT. (2.4 M)!

PS: EVEN IF YOU ARE BEST FRIENDS
WITH A GRIFFIN, DO NOT COME
NEAR IT WHEN IT IS HUNGRY! A
GRIFFIN'S TALONS ARE KNOWN TO
BE SUPER SHARP. IF A GRIFFIN
WANTS SOME GRUB, IT CAN EASILY
GRAB HOLD OF LARGE ANIMALS
SUCH AS HUMANS, HORSES, OR EVEN
ELEPHANTS! ONCE IT GRABS HOLD
OF ITS PREY, IT FLIES HIGH INTO THE
SKY, AND THEN DROPS THE PREY TO
ITS DEATH. OUCH!

Ӿ FURRY, MUSCLED BODY
OF A LION

Ӿ HIND LEGS OF
A LION

Ӿ TAIL OF A LION

SOMETIMES THE
TAIL LOOKS LIKE
A SNAKE!

Griffin Eggs

Griffin eggs are about the
same height as a banana.
In medieval times, people
were willing to pay big
bucks for griffin's eggs,
eager to raise their own
griffin as they would a
horse. Griffins often laid
their eggs in deep, dark
caves with very narrow
entrances to shelter the
eggs from harsh
weather and
deadly predators!

11

THE GRIFFIN'S
PERSONALITY AND MAGIC

Known to be a courageous, loyal, wise, and magical being, a griffin's personality is second to no other beast of its time. Let's take a closer look.

EVER DREAM ABOUT FLYING ON THE BACK OF A GRIFFIN? FIRST YOU MUST SHOW YOU ARE NOT A THREAT, AND YOU MUST ALSO IMPRESS IT! WHAT WOULD YOU DO TO IMPRESS A GRIFFIN?

COOL, CALM, AND COURAGEOUS

A griffin could stand up to the worst of the worst supervillains. Nothing scares the griffin. Its courage stems from a deep desire to keep safe whatever it is protecting. In many cases, a griffin would rather die than give in to an enemy. It has the power to stick through a fight for as long as takes to guarantee victory, where other beasts might not be able to last in battle as long.

EVERLASTING LOYALTY

Griffins only guard treasure for people they consider very special. It's rare for a griffin to be close with another creature or human. If you are lucky enough to gain a griffin's friendship, that means you have earned its trust and it will do anything for you! So, dragon, beware: the griffin cares as much about defending its friends as it does about protecting its treasure. **Loyalty is extra motivation for a griffin to fight until the battle is won!**

WISDOM

The griffin can be a jokester and silly beast, like its pal, the sphinx. (Check out the next page to read about the sphinx.) It often uses its wit—speaking in riddles or asking difficult questions—to fend off less intelligent visitors. Again and again, the griffin chooses smarts over strength in a battle, planning and practicing **strategies of attack** and special moves that would easily defeat an intruder. But can the griffin outwit a dragon?

MAGIC MANIA

Griffin Claws

Griffin claws change color when they come in contact with poison. In medieval times, people would drink from griffin-claw goblets to make sure they were not being poisoned.

Griffin Feathers

Griffin feathers cure sickness and even blindness! So why hasn't your doctor prescribed you griffin feathers when you are sick? Because they are extremely rare and difficult to come across. If he or she were fortunate enough to find one, they may be tempted to keep it for themselves.

TYPES OF GRIFFINS

The original griffin is a unique beast, but there are other magical and mysterious creatures that share similar characteristics. Perhaps one of these distant relatives would come to the griffin's aid if it is attacked!

HIPPOGRIFF

A hippogriff has the head, talons, and wings of an eagle, just like a griffin. But instead of lion parts, it has the hind legs, body, and tail of a horse.

HIPPOGRIFFS ARE EXTREMELY FAST CREATURES! THEY CAN OUTRUN AND OUTFLY A DRAGON IN A HEARTBEAT.

WHEN A HIPPOGRIFF LOSES A FEATHER, THE FEATHER BECOMES INVISIBLE. IF YOU FOUND HIPPOGRIFF FEATHERS, YOU COULD MAKE A CLOAK THAT WOULD ALLOW YOU TO GO ANYWHERE WITHOUT ANYONE SEEING YOU!

sphinx is often found guarding spectacular treasure. The most well-known sphinx is the Great Sphinx of Giza.

ROC

A roc is a huge bird rumored to be so strong that it can grab

an elephant from the ground. This beast is so big that it has been mistaken for a floating mountain!

PEGASUS

A pegasus has large feathered wings and the head, body, and legs of a horse. A creature in Greek mythology, a pegasus flew all the way from Earth to **Mount Olympus**. Zeus, king of the gods, was so impressed by the pegasus, that he allowed it to carry his lightning bolts.

SPHINX

A sphinx has a human head and the body of a lion, and some have wings. A sphinx has a silly personality. It loves riddles! Like the griffin, the

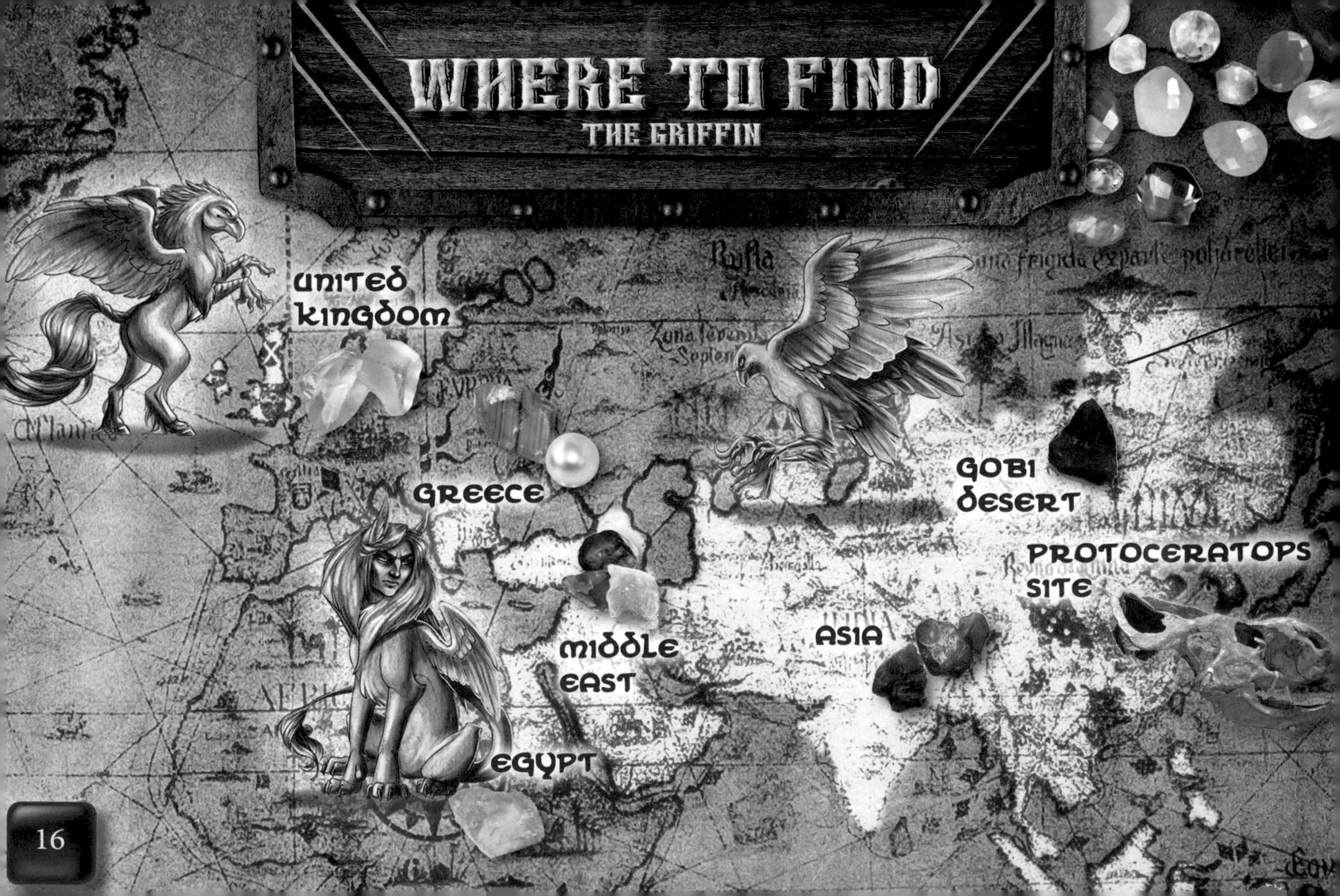

WHERE TO FIND

THE GRIFFIN

UNITED
KINGDOM

GREECE

MIDDLE
EAST

EGYPT

GOBI
DESERT

PROTOCERATOPS
SITE

ASIA

If you are going on a griffin hunt or you wish to find where this battle will most likely take place, it might not be as easy as you would hope. Remember, griffins have wings, so their nests are very high up, usually out of sight. Make sure to bring binoculars or a telescope.

Griffins can live anywhere in the world! But you are more likely to find them in the Gobi Desert, the Middle East, Asia, Greece, and the United Kingdom, because those places are known to have a large assortment of gems and precious metals!

They generally live high in the mountains in a nest, which is sometimes made of gold and laced with gems. The nests are often on top of tall, craggy rocks or at the edge of cliffs so that they can easily see intruders attempting to climb up and steal their treasure.

If a griffin is not in a nest, then it is most likely in a cave up high with a very narrow entrance, especially if the griffin plans on laying eggs.

DINOSAUR BONES VS. GRIFFIN BONES

Bones that resemble a griffin's were recently found near gold veins in the Gobi Desert! These bones have actually been identified as a dinosaur known as the Protoceratops. But what do you think: is it a dinosaur or griffin skull?

WHERE DO YOU THINK THIS BATTLE WILL TAKE PLACE, IN A CAVE OR UP HIGH IN A NEST?

WARNING!

Unlike a griffin, a dragon cannot be impressed. It is a ruthless warrior, willing to do whatever it takes to get what it wants.

DO NOT GET IN ITS WAY.

THE MIGHTY DRAGON

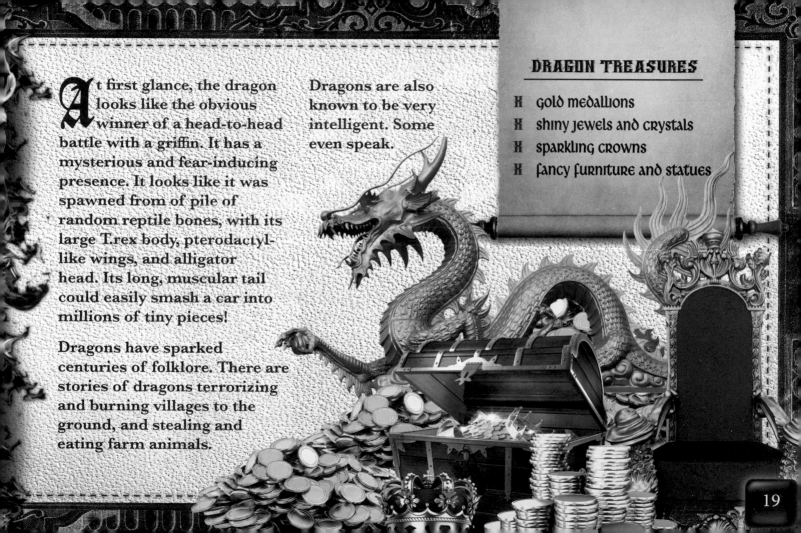

At first glance, the dragon looks like the obvious winner of a head-to-head battle with a griffin. It has a mysterious and fear-inducing presence. It looks like it was spawned from of pile of random reptile bones, with its large T.rex body, pterodactyl-like wings, and alligator head. Its long, muscular tail could easily smash a car into millions of tiny pieces!

Dragons have sparked centuries of folklore. There are stories of dragons terrorizing and burning villages to the ground, and stealing and eating farm animals.

Dragons are also known to be very intelligent. Some even speak.

DRAGON TREASURES

- H gold medallions
- H shiny jewels and crystals
- H sparkling crowns
- H fancy furniture and statues

19

LEGENDS OF THE DRAGON

The dragon is famous and known around the world for its strength, size, and quick temper. For hundreds of years, humans have feared possible encounters with dragons on their journeys to unknown lands, and very few have lived to tell the tale of a dragon encounter.

KNIGHTS AND MEDIEVAL LEGENDS

The most famous tale from medieval times is the legend of King Arthur of Camelot and a wizard named Merlin. There are two dragons in this magical story, one red and one white. They represent two kingdoms and their intense hatred for one another.

GREEK AND ROMAN MYTHOLOGY

In ancient Greece, there were many different deadly dragons! One dragon was tasked to guard an orchard of magical golden apples! Another dragon guarded a golden fleece, which is basically a fur coat. This fleece was a symbol of kingly authority.

NORSE MYTHOLOGY

Vikings were almost as fierce and fearless as dragons. They pillaged, destroyed, and stole land. They also spread stories about ferocious dragons to scare the people they attacked.

Believing that the dragon could grant them special protection, the Vikings attached wood-carved dragon heads to the fronts and backs of their ships.

OTHER POPULAR STORIES WITH DRAGONS

- Harry Potter
- Lord of the Rings
- The Chronicles of Narnia
- Alice Through the Looking Glass
- Beowulf

DRAGONS CAN THROW THE BEST BBQS!

Dragons can live to be hundreds of years old. Think about it this way: when a dragon is 100 years old, it's still considered to be young—practically a teenager in dragon years! But when a human is 100 years old, we usually have white hair and walking sticks! On average, a dragon grows to be about 30 ft. (9 m) tall—the size of a two-story house!

A DRAGON'S THICK, SCALY SKIN IS ITS BEST KEPT SECRET! WHY, YOU ASK? BECAUSE IT'S SO STRONG AND TOUGH, IT SERVES AS THE DRAGON'S OWN NATURAL ARMOR! TRY PUTTING A SWORD OR ARROW THROUGH IT AND IT WILL BOUNCE OFF LIKE A BASKETBALL HITTING THE BACKBOARD.

✗ FEROCIOUS FANGS

✗ LIZARD-LIKE BODY

A DRAGON'S TAIL IS STRONGER THAN ITS ARMS! SOMETIMES THE END OF ITS TAIL IS SHAPED LIKE AN ARROWHEAD, WITH SHARP SPIKES ON IT, OR—CRAZIEST OF ALL—IT CONTAINS POISONOUS VENOM!

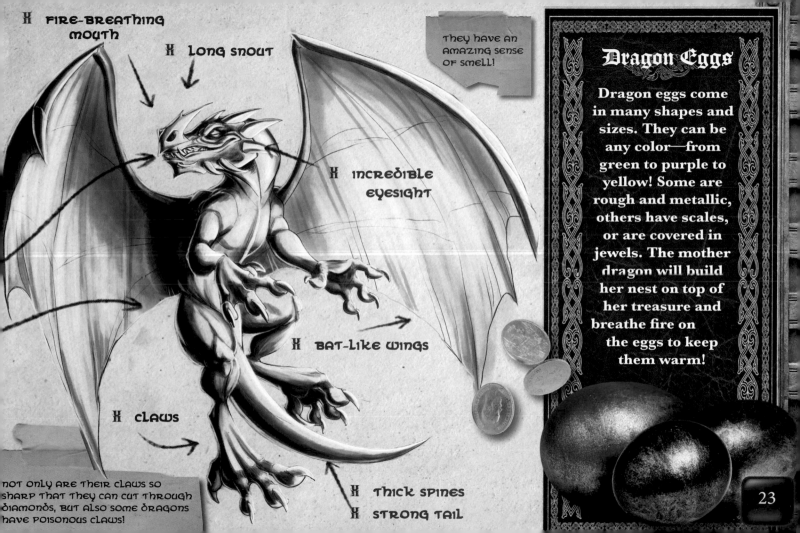

FIRE-BREATHING MOUTH

LONG SNOUT

THEY HAVE AN AMAZING SENSE OF SMELL!

INCREDIBLE EYESIGHT

BAT-LIKE WINGS

CLAWS

NOT ONLY ARE THEIR CLAWS SO SHARP THAT THEY CAN CUT THROUGH DIAMONDS, BUT ALSO SOME DRAGONS HAVE POISONOUS CLAWS!

THICK SPINES

STRONG TAIL

Dragon Eggs

Dragon eggs come in many shapes and sizes. They can be any color—from green to purple to yellow! Some are rough and metallic, others have scales, or are covered in jewels. The mother dragon will build her nest on top of her treasure and breathe fire on the eggs to keep them warm!

23

THE DRAGON'S
PERSONALITY AND MAGIC

TREASURE THIEF

Do not leave your shiny, valuable objects unattended, because in some myths dragons are greedy monsters. Their greed can lead them to do violent and terrible things. Their quest for treasure never ends.

WISE~GUY DRAGON

In some myths, dragons are revered for their wisdom. They are so wise and intelligent that they taught humans how to speak! In these myths, dragons are also known for their goodness.

MAGIC MANIA

X fire-breathing beast: we know some dragons breathe fire. but did you know some also breathe snow or ice? burr!

X mysterious mind control: if you cross paths with a dragon with this power, it could mean immediate surrender, death, or—worse—torture!

- ᚻ dragon tongue: grants the ability to win any argument
- ᚻ dragon heart: turns a person into a genius
- ᚻ dragon fat: rub some of this on you and it will keep away vicious beasts
- ᚻ dragon blood: heals wounds, makes a person invincible, grants long life, or gives a person a higher level of intelligence
- ᚻ camouflage: much like a chameleon, some dragons can change colors to help them blend in with their backgrounds. they use this power to protect themselves or to sneak up on an enemy
- ᚻ dragon teeth: are you in need of an army? well, have no fear! plant a few dragon teeth and mighty warriors will grow!

TYPES OF DRAGONS

HYDRA

A hydra is a multiheaded monster! If one head is cut off, one or two more will grow back in its place, which makes it almost impossible to defeat. Some hydras have poisonous breath and blood that can kill instantly.

KNUCKER

In the heart of a dark and smelly swamp or damp hole called a knuckerhole, you might find a creepy, giant knucker dragon. It has wings and sometimes shoots venom that can liquefy its prey!

WANT TO KNOW SOMETHING COOL? IF A WARRIOR CAN GET HIS HANDS ON HYDRA BLOOD, HE CAN DIP HIS ARROWS INTO THE BLOOD. THE BLOOD THEN MAKES HIS ARROWS AN EVEN MORE DEADLY WEAPON WHEN FIRED AT AN ENEMY.

MANY LEGENDS OF THE KNUCKER DRAGON STEM FROM SUSSEX, ENGLAND.

IN NORSE MYTHOLOGY, THE LINDWORM IS THE ARCHENEMY OF THE MIGHTY NORSE GOD AND POPULAR SUPERHERO, THOR.

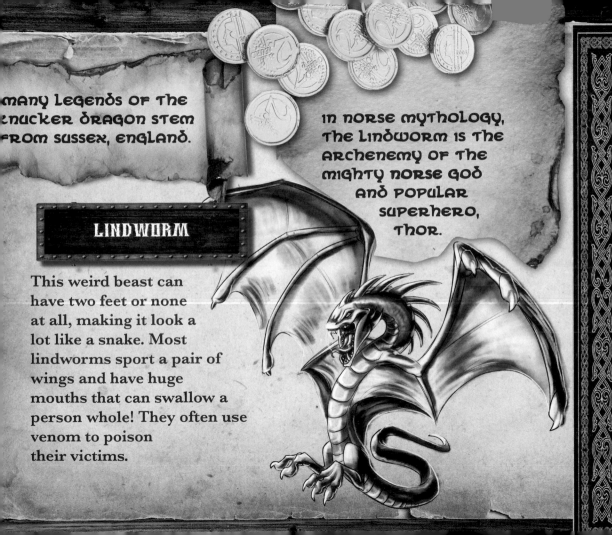

LINDWORM

This weird beast can have two feet or none at all, making it look a lot like a snake. Most lindworms sport a pair of wings and have huge mouths that can swallow a person whole! They often use venom to poison their victims.

Poisoned Pie

Beware! This is one delicious looking pie that will destroy you! Legend says a farmer boy killed a knucker dragon by making a poisoned pie and leaving the pie outside of its knuckerhole. The dragon ate the pie and died from the poison. Then the farmer boy returned and cut off the dragon's head!

WHERE TO FIND
THE DRAGON

UNITED KINGDOM

GERMANY

GREECE

MIDDLE EAST

ASIA

If you want to go on a gallant quest to find a dragon, it's best to start where the legend began, in Rome and Greece, and then travel through Germany, France, and the United Kingdom. Dragons can also be found in parts of Asia and the Middle East.

LONG AGO, CARTOGRAPHERS WOULD DRAW DRAGONS AND OTHER MYTHICAL CREATURES ON PARTS OF MAPS DEPICTING UNEXPLORED AREAS, EXPRESSING THE COMMON FEAR PEOPLE SHARED DURING THOSE TIMES OF EXPLORING UNKNOWN LANDS AND SEAS.

Dragons make their homes in all sorts of hidden, shadowy areas:

- caves and lairs by the seaside
- dense and dark forests
- murky and misty swamps and lakes
- in the middle of mysterious mountains

Most of the time, dragons choose caves because they like the cooler temperatures. A cave also brings them closer to natural crystals and gems, which makes this treasure hunter feel right at home.

DINOSAUR BONES VS. DRAGON BONES

In 1335, when the skull of a woolly rhinoceros was found in a cave near Klagenfurt, Germany, it was believed to be a dragon's skull. What do you think: is it a dinosaur or dragon skull?

29

GRIFFIN AND DRAGON

GRIFFIN

power	■■□
technique	■■■■□
patience	■■■■□
balance	■■■□
sight	■■■□
hearing	■■■■□
size	■■□
intelligence	■■■■□
flight speed	■■■□

power move:
talon grab
combo move:
talon grab and beak punch
special advantage:
fight is on its home turf

Physically, a griffin doesn't
measure up to the larger,
stronger dragon, but its
higher level of intelligence,
patience, and technique
gives it has a good chance
at victory by outwitting and
outlasting the dragon.

HEAD~TO~HEAD

DRAGON

power move:

fire breath

combo move:

fire breath and tale whip

special advantage:

surprise attack

Overall, the dragon is more powerful than the griffin because of its size and strength. It is also unpredictable: it could do one crazy, savage move and win the fight immediately.

				power
				technique
				patience
				balance
				sight
				hearing
				size
				intelligence
				flight speed

31

WHY THE GRIFFIN
COULD WIN

READY, SET, ATTACK!

BRING IT!

The battle has begun! The griffin has one job to do: protect its treasure! The griffin is a determined beast. It will not shy away from the large and powerful dragon that has disturbed its nesting ground.

The griffin has planned for a moment just like this. This isn't the first time a greedy beast has tried to steal its treasure.

The dragon has wandered onto the griffin's home turf. The dragon does not know the immediate surroundings as well as the griffin, so the griffin can use that to its advantage.

Maintaining focus is the griffin's greatest strength. It does not even blink an eye! It watches, listens, and outwits the dragon as the dragon strikes. Mustering up its strength of a hundred eagles, the griffin waits for the right moment to rip the dragon's flesh with its razor-sharp talons and then pluck out its eyes with its powerful beak. If a dragon can't see, how will it know where the treasure is?

FIGHT FOR LIFE!

32

The fight has only just begun, but the griffin is confident and motivated to win! It is ready to fight to the death, and it will not go down without making the dragon pay for its greed.

VICTORY IS MINE!

WHY THE DRAGON
COULD WIN

The dragon surprises the griffin by entering into the nesting area with a loud roar and fire spewing from its mouth! It takes advantage of its size and speed and immediately knocks the griffin from its nest.

The dragon can tell that the griffin is calculating its every move. But using its strong muscular tail, it swipes and thrashes at the griffin in hopes it will distract its foe. The dragon continues to blow huge blazes of fire, keeping the griffin at a distance while it accomplishes the task at hand—stealing the treasure!

The griffin, frustratingly smart, has found a way around the fire and the tail, and it attempts to attack the dragon's flesh. The dragon can sense that the griffin is caught off guard by the dragon's thick and protective skin. The dragon laughs and slams the confused griffin into the side of a cliff.

GIVE ME EVERYTHING YOU'VE GOT!

The dragon is getting tired. It's ready to make one final move to end this! Is the griffin doomed, or will it struggle free and keep fighting for the win?

down with the griffin!

CRAFTING YOUR BEAST
GRIFFIN

Use your clay and the steps below to craft your own gifted griffin and prepare him for a face-off with the mighty dragon.

1 Pick a clay color you think best fits your griffin and roll it into a ball that is as big as its chest. Flatten the ball into a square.

2 Wrap the square around the griffin's ribs and shoulders like a jacket. Press clay onto the skeleton so that it sticks, but leave the hole where the wings go uncovered.

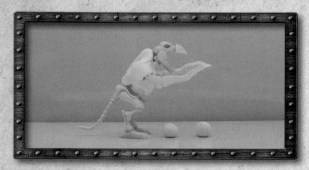

3 Now pinch off one small piece of clay and roll it into a ball. Work the ball onto your griffin's front leg until it is covered. Do the same for all four legs.

5 It's time to cover that long tail. Grab some clay and roll it into a snake. Make sure your snake is as long as the griffin's tail.

4 To cover the head, pinch off another piece of clay, about the size of the griffin's head, and roll it into a ball. Use your fingers to move the clay around until the head is covered.

6 Take the snake and lay it on top of the tail. Work the clay around the tail until it's covered.

$\mathcal{I}$t's all in the details! To make your griffin extra fierce, use one of the other clay colors to add accents for the griffin's wings, claws, tail, beak, eyes, and mane.

8 Claws: Pinch off twelve very small pieces of clay. Roll them into tiny rounded ovals. Place three ovals on each of the griffin's four paws.

7 Roll out a long, thin snake. Using the width of the wing for reference, measure out a piece of the clay snake that matches the width of wing. Press in. Repeat until whole wing is covered in rolls of clay. For wing edges, roll out long, thin snake of another clay color and press in around wing edges for accent.

9 Beak: Roll two small pieces of clay into balls and flatten each like pancakes. Place one pancake on the top front the griffin's mouth and wrap it around. Do the same for the lower jaw.

10 Eyes: Roll two little clay balls. Press each ball where you think the eyes should go.

Adding wings to the griffin body

While the clay is still moist and pliable, push the wings into the holes that were left exposed at the beginning of your build. Use a little more clay to smooth out the area between the body and wing, so that it is sure to stick.

11 Mane: Roll a long thin snake and break it up into ten tiny snakes attach them one by one, stack them and layering them on the back of the griffin's head.

A MYTHICAL MASTERPIECE
YOUR CLAY GRIFFIN

Here are some fantastical clay mockups demonstrating a few options on how to use the glaze to customize your griffin.

✱ ONE COOL WAY TO CUSTOMIZE YOUR GRIFFIN IS TO DIP THE PAINTBRUSH IN THE GOLD METALLIC GLAZE AND APPLY IT CAREFULLY ALONG THE ACCENT AREAS AS PICTURED TO THE RIGHT.

40

✗ YOU CAN ALSO GO FOR A FULL-COVERAGE LOOK BY LIBERALLY APPLYING GLAZE TO THE GRIFFIN'S WHOLE BODY.

CRAFTING YOUR BEAST
DRAGON

se your clay and the steps below to craft your own mighty dragon and prepare him for a face-off with the gifted griffin.

1 Since you've already picked the main color for your griffin, try using the other color for the main body of the dragon. Pull off a piece of clay that is about the size of the griffin's chest, and roll it into a ball. Flatten the ball into a square.

2 Wrap the square around the dragon's ribs and shoulders like a jacket. Press clay onto the skeleton so that it sticks, but leave the hole where the wings go uncovered.

3 Roll four small pieces of clay into balls. Push the first ball onto your dragon's front leg until it is covered. Repeat for all four legs.

5 It's time to cover the tail. Grab some clay and roll it into a snake. Make sure your snake is as long as the dragon's tail.

4 To cover the head, pinch off another piece of clay, about the size of the dragon's head and roll it into a ball. Use your fingers to work the clay around the head until it is covered.

6 Take the snake and lay it on top of the tail. Work the clay around the tail until it's covered.

It's all in the details! To make your dragon look more powerful, use one of the other clay colors to add accents for its spine, tail, horns, claws, eyes, brows, and wings.

8 Spine and tail: Pinch off some clay. Roll out a long, thin snake. Place the snake on the back of the dragon from the base of its head to the tip of its tail. Grab a toothpick and press it along the tail to form evenly spaced ridges.

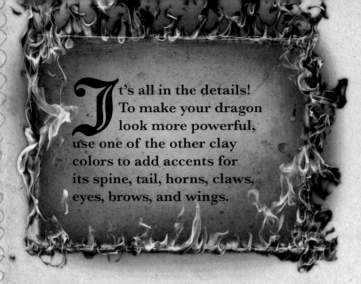

7 Wings: Roll up a medium-sized clay ball and flatten. Then use your fingers to spread the clay over the wing covering all the ridges and tips.

9 Horns: Roll five small balls of clay and place on the five horns pinching them on the tips to make them appear sharp and dangerous.

10 Claws: Pinch off sixteen very small pieces of clay. Roll them into tiny rounded ovals. Place three ovals on the front each of the dragon's digits and one on the back.

11 Eyes/brows: Roll two small clay balls. Press each ball where the eyes go. Next roll two small, thin snakes. Apply them above the eyes and shape to form brows.

12 Wings: Roll a long, thin snake and split it in half. Take one half and press it along the length of the outside of the wing—from tip to tip. Take the second snake, split it in half, and press each half onto one of the interior lines of the wing. Do the same for the other wing.

Adding wings to the dragon body

With clay still moist, push wings into holes left open at the beginning of the build. Smooth clay around wing joints.

A MYTHICAL MASTERPIECE
YOUR MIGHTY CLAY DRAGON

Here are some fantastical clay mockups demonstrating a few options on how to use the glaze to customize your dragon.

※ ONE COOL WAY TO CUSTOMIZE YOUR ÐRAGON IS TO ÐIP THE PAINT BRUSH IN THE GOLÐ METALLIC GLAZE AND APPLY IT CAREFULLY ALONG THE ACCENT AREAS AS PICTUREÐ TO THE RIGHT.

✗ YOU CAN ALSO GO FOR A FULL-COVERAGE LOOK BY LIBERALLY APPLYING THE GLAZE TO THE DRAGON'S WHOLE BODY.

GLOSSARY

CARTOGRAPHER: someone who makes maps

DIVINE: godly, of great power

EMBLEM: a device, symbol, or figure used as an identifying mark

FLEECE: the fur coat of an animal

IMMORTAL: live forever

LOYALTY: strong sense of support or friendship

MEDIEVAL: European history between the 5th and 15th centuries

MOUNT OLYMPUS: in mythology, a mountain where the Greek gods and goddesses lived

MYTHOLOGICAL: relating to a legendary story that is not true

NORSE: stemming from northern Germany

STRATEGIES: carefully designed plans

VIKING: a pirate from Scandinavia, who lived between the 8th and 11th centuries